P9-CAO-787

Meet a Baby Lion

Samantha S. Bell

Lerner Publications
Minneapolis

Content Consultant: Dr. Mark C. Andersen, Department of Fish Wildlife and Conservation Ecology, New Mexico State University

Lerner Publications Company
A division of Lerner Publishing Group, Inc.
241 First Avenue North
Minneapolis, MN 55401 USA

For reading levels and more information, look up this title at www.lernerbooks.com.

Cataloging-in-Publication Data for *Meet a Baby Lion* is on file at the Library of Congress.
ISBN: 978-1-4677-7974-6 (lib.)
ISBN: 978-1-4677-8367-5 (pbk.)
ISBN: 978-1-4677-8368-2 (EB pdf)

Manufactured in the United States of America
1 – BP – 7/15/15

Table of Contents

At Home in the Den

A mother lion rests in her hidden den. She has just given birth to two lion cubs. The cubs are blind and need their mother.

A mother lion licks her newborn cubs.

Newborn cubs grow quickly.

Each newborn cub weighs about 3 pounds (1 kilogram). That's as much as four storybooks. The cubs will grow to weigh up to 500 pounds (227 kg), or as much as a small piano!

Lions have a litter of one to six cubs at a time.

The cubs are tan like their mother.

Cubs have dark spots on their heads and legs.

Male lions will grow a mane as they get bigger.

Also like their mother, cubs don't have a bushy mane. Only adult male lions have a mane.

The mother is part of a group called a pride. There are twelve to forty female lions in the pride. They are mothers, aunts, daughters, and sisters.

Most lions in a pride are from the same family.

Soon these cubs will join the pride too.

There are also one to three male lions in the pride.

These males are not related.

Part of the Pride

The mother lion's den may be a cave or a group of bushes called a thicket. She moves her cubs from den to den.

Switching dens makes it hard for predators to find cubs.

A mother lion keeps her cubs close by.

Mother lions need to be careful. Hyenas, jackals, and leopards kill baby lions. Eagles, snakes, and

Lion cubs grow fast. They open their eyes during the first week. By two weeks old, the cubs can walk.

Cubs can run at four weeks old.

Cubs join the pride when they are old enough.

When the cubs are about eight weeks old, the mother lion brings them to the pride.

Cubs nurse until they are about nine months old.

Newborn cubs drink their mothers' milk. After the cubs join the pride, other mother lions also nurse them.

The baby lions play with other cubs and adult lions. They stalk and chase rocks. They pounce on sticks. They are learning how to hunt.

Cubs pounce on rocks and logs!

Born to Hunt

Lions eat any meat they can find. They catch small animals such as birds and reptiles.

Cubs sometimes eat the prey their parents hunted and caught.

They eat large animals such as zebras, giraffes, and wildebeests. They even eat animals that other predators have killed.

Zebras are just one of the animals lions hunt.

Cubs learn to hunt by watching the adults catch prey.

The cubs start eating meat when they are three months old. When the cubs are eleven months old, they are ready to join the hunt. They follow behind the adult lions and watch.

Lions hunt at night alone or in groups. Usually the females hunt, but sometimes the males will help.

Male lions are stronger than females and can catch larger animals.

19

When an animal is caught, the lions in the pride share the meal. The male lions eat first. They need at least 15 pounds (7 kg) of meat each day. That's as much as 150 hot dogs.

Males eat first since they must eat the most.

When the males are finished, the females have a turn. Females need 11 pounds (5 kg) or more of meat each day. The cubs eat what is left.

On the Plains

Lions live on grassy plains, savannas, and open woodlands. Each pride has its own territory.

Lions let others know where their territory is by roaring.

When male lions are about three years old, they leave the pride. The young males roam until they are bigger.

A young male roams an African plain.

When the young male lions are about five years old, they fight other lions to try to take over another pride. If they win, the other males must leave.

Males fight for control of a pride.

Males begin their own families when they join a new pride.

At the age of five, the new males mate with the females in the pride and have cubs of their own. They stay until a stronger male lion comes along.

Grown male lions are about 6 feet (2 m) long, or as long as a couch. Female lions are a little shorter.

Male lions grow to be strong and powerful.

Male lions live for only about twelve years because they often fight one another. Female lions live between fifteen and eighteen years.

Lion Life Cycle

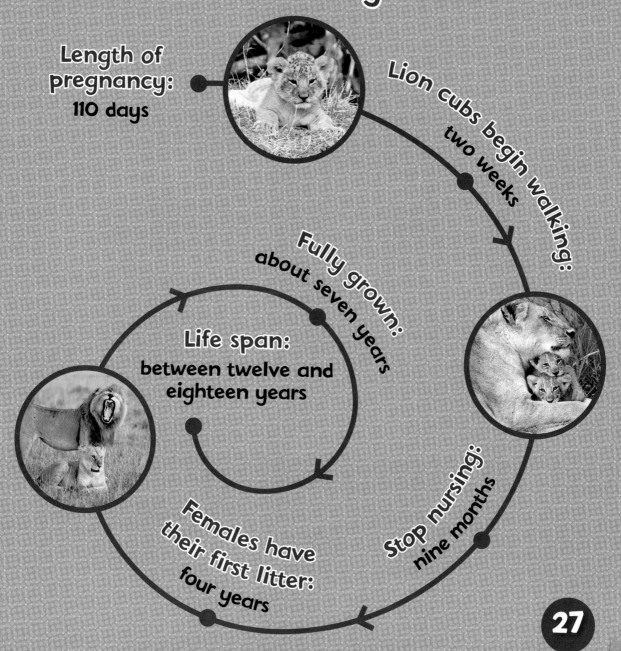

Length of pregnancy: 110 days

Lion cubs begin walking: two weeks

Fully grown: about seven years

Life span: between twelve and eighteen years

Stop nursing: nine months

Females have their first litter: four years

Habitat in Focus

- Lions live on grassy plains, savannas, and open woodlands. They can hide in the long grass and creep up on their prey.

- The average size of a pride's territory is 40 to 50 square miles (104 to 130 square kilometers).

- Farmers raise goats and cattle in lion habitats. Sometimes, lions attack the livestock, so the farmers kill the lions.

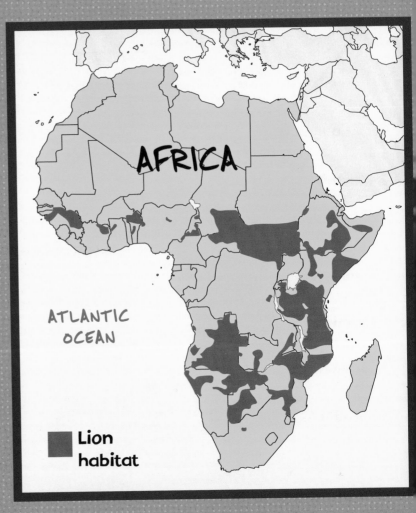

AFRICA

ATLANTIC OCEAN

Lion habitat

Fun Facts

- Both male and female lions roar.

- A lion's roar can be heard from more than 5 miles (8 km) away.

- Lions sleep twenty hours each day.

- A lion's mane gets longer and darker with age.

- Lions can run at speeds up to 50 miles (81 km) per hour.

- White lions live in South Africa.

Glossary

hyena: a large animal of Africa that eats the flesh of dead animals

jackal: a wild dog found in Africa

nurse: to drink milk from a female

predator: an animal that hunts and kills other animals for food

roam: to go from place to place

savanna: African grassland

stalk: to hunt quietly and slowly

thicket: a thick patch of shrubbery, underbrush, or small trees

wildebeest: a large antelope with a head like an ox and horns that curve downward

woodland: land covered with trees and shrubs

Further Reading

Anderson, Sheila. *What Can Live in a Grassland?* Minneapolis: Lerner Publications, 2011.

Blewett, Ashlee Brown. *Mission: Lion Rescue.* Washington, DC: National Geographic Kids, 2014.

Carney, Elizabeth. *National Geographic Kids Everything Big Cats.* Washington, DC: National Geographic, 2011.

Fort Wayne Children's Zoo: African Lion
http://kidszoo.org/our-animals/african-journey/african-lion

National Geographic Kids: Lion
http://kids.nationalgeographic.com/content/kids/en_US/animals/lion

San Diego Zoo Kids: African Lion
http://kids.sandiegozoo.org/animals/mammals/african-lion

Index

Photo Acknowledgments

The images in this book are used with the permission of: © Peter Betts/Shutterstock Images, pp. 2, 23; © Images of Africa Photobank/Alamy, p. 4; © Cuc80/iStock/Thinkstock, pp. 5, 27 (top); © Dave Pusey/Shutterstock Images, pp. 6, 27 (bottom right); © Dennis W. Donohue/Shutterstock Images, p. 7; © Stuart G. Porter/Shutterstock Images, p. 8; © moizhusein/Shutterstock Images, pp. 9, 20; © Ariadne Van Zandbergen/Alamy, p. 10; © KA Photography KEVM111/Shutterstock Images, p. 11; © Jake Sorensen/Shutterstock Images, pp. 12, 31; © Anton Ivanov/Shutterstock Images, p. 13; © webguzs/iStock/Thinkstock, p. 14; © J. Reineke/Shutterstock Images, p. 15; © Diane Diederich/iStock/Thinkstock, p. 16; © Africanway/iStock/Thinkstock, p. 17; © Galyna Andrushko/Shutterstock Images, p. 18; © Alta Oosthuizen/Shutterstock Images, p. 19; © Nick Biemans/Shutterstock Images, p. 21; © Gautham Manohar/Shutterstock Images, pp. 22, 27 (bottom left); © Aditya "Dicky" Singh/Alamy, p. 24; © pum eva/iStock/Thinkstock, p. 25; © TanzanianImages/iStock/Thinkstock, p. 26; Red Line Editorial, 28; © GlobalP/iStock/Thinkstock, p. 30.

Front cover: © iStockphoto.com/StuPorts.

Main body text set in Johann Light 30/36.